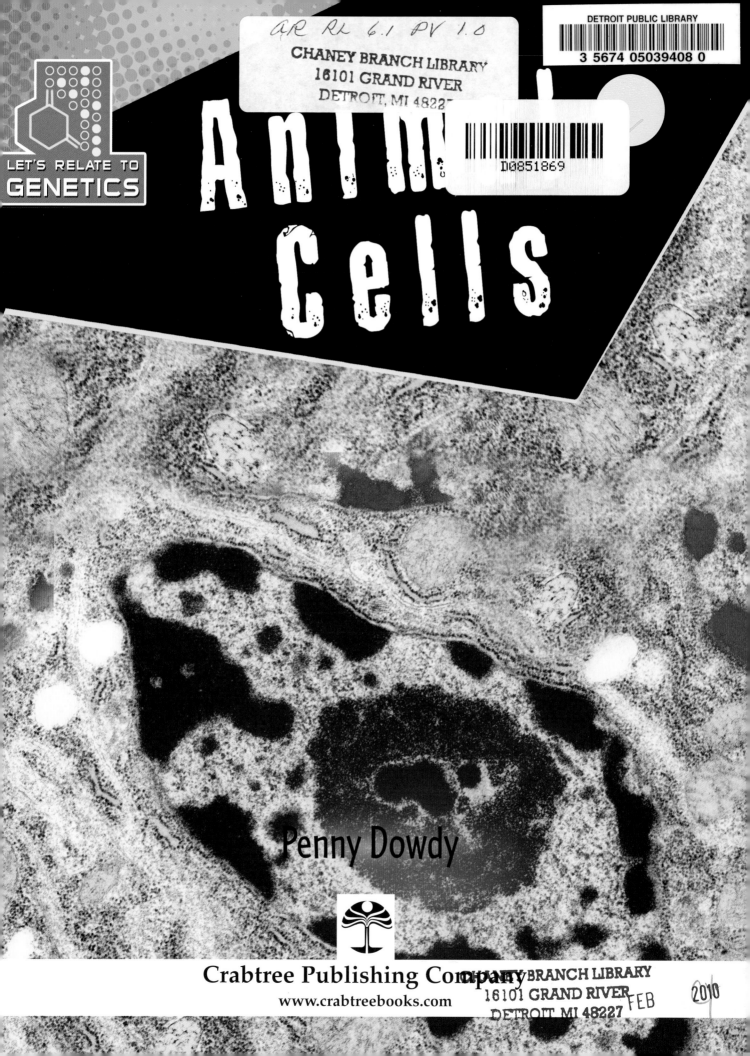

LET'S RELATE TO
GENETICS

Animal Cells

Penny Dowdy

Crabtree Publishing Company
www.crabtreebooks.com

Crabtree Publishing Company

www.crabtreebooks.com

Author: Penny Dowdy
Coordinating editor: Chester Fisher
Series editor: Jessica Cohn
Editorial director: Kathy Middleton
Editor: Adrianna Morganelli
Production coordinator: Katherine Berti
Prepress technician: Katherine Berti
Project manager: Kumar Kunal (Q2AMEDIA)
Art direction: Harleen Mehta (Q2AMEDIA)
Cover design: Tarang Saggar (Q2AMEDIA)
Design: Ritu Chopra, Rohit Juneja (Q2AMEDIA)
Photo research: Mariea Janet (Q2AMEDIA)

Photographs:
123RF: Mark Rasmussen: p. 16
Associated Press: Jim Mone: p. 41
Corbis: Visuals Unlimited: p. 1, 33 (top); Bettmann: p. 7, 9, 11 (left);
   Joe McDonald: p. 10; Visuals Unlimited: p. 23 (bottom)
Dreamstime: Dreamstime: p. 13 (left), 40; Vasilis Akoinoglou: p. 22;
   Tatiana Morozova: p. 26; Jennifer Boyd: p. 27 (bottom); Dennis Sabo:
   p. 30; Adam Goss: p. 38; Utekhina Anna: p. 39; Andres Rodriguez: p. 42
Fotolia: Martin Green: p. 23 (top): Fotolia: p. 24; Vanessa: p. 25 (left),
   28-29; Sonya Etchison: p. 32
Getty Images: Stephen Schauer/The Image Bank: p. 13 (right); Joe
   McDonald/Visuals Unlimited: p. 27 (top)
Istockphoto: Steve Boyle/NewSport/Corbis, Parpalea Catalin: cover;
   Jakub Semeniuk: p. 12; Doug Schneider: p. 17; Damir Spanic:
   p. 19 (bottom); Istockphoto: p. 44 (top)
Photolibrary: Ed Reschke: p. 6; Mary Evans Picture Library: p. 8;
   Matt Carr: p. 34; Jamie Tanaka: p. 37
Reuters: Phil McCarten: p. 4; Ho Old: p. 5
Science Photo Library: Revy, Ism: p. 14-15; Thomas Deerinck, Ncmir: p. 15
Shutterstock: Kirsty Pargeter: p. 11 (right); Tatiana Morozova: p. 18;
   Rémi Cauzid: p. 19 (top); Darren Baker: p. 20; Sebastian Kaulitzki:
   p. 25 (right), 33 (bottom); Diak: p. 31 (top); Ivan Cholakov Gostock:
   p. 31 (bottom); Lepas: p. 35; Patrick Hall: p. 36; Zany Zeus: p. 43;
   Foong Kok Leong: p. 44 (bottom); Shutterstock: p. 45
Q2AMedia Art Bank: p. 21 45

Cover:
Main image:
   Bred to be fast and agile, Thoroughbred horses combine
   the genes of English mares and Arabian stallions.
Inset image:
   When a sea star loses a limb, it can grow a new
   one thanks to cell division.
What makes a tiger striped?:
   Hair cells are actually dead cells that have been bound
   with a protein called keratin. The color in a tiger's stripe
   comes from the pigment cells found in the middle and
   outer layers of the hair shaft.

Library and Archives Canada Cataloguing in Publication

Dowdy, Penny
   Animal cells / Penny Dowdy.

(Let's relate to genetics)
Includes index.
ISBN 978-0-7787-4947-9 (bound).--ISBN 978-0-7787-4964-6 (pbk.)

   1. Cells--Juvenile literature. 2. Cytology--Juvenile literature.
I. Title. II. Series: Let's relate to genetics

QH582.5.D69 2009   j571.6'1   C2009-903981-8

Library of Congress Cataloging-in-Publication Data

Dowdy, Penny.
   Animal cells / Penny Dowdy.
      p. cm. -- (Let's relate to genetics)
   Includes index.
   ISBN 978-0-7787-4947-9 (reinforced lib. bdg. : alk. paper)
   -- ISBN 978-0-7787-4964-6 (pbk. : alk. paper)
   1. Animal cell biotechnology--Juvenile literature. I. Title. II. Series.

TP248.27.A53D69 2010
660.6'5--dc22
                                                    2009025290

Crabtree Publishing Company

www.crabtreebooks.com   1-800-387-7650

Published in Canada
Crabtree Publishing
616 Welland Ave.
St. Catharines, ON
L2M 5V6

Published in the United States
Crabtree Publishing
PMB16A
350 Fifth Ave., Suite 3308
New York, NY 10118

Published in the United Kingdom
Crabtree Publishing
Maritime House
Basin Road North, Hove
BN41 1WR

Published in Australia
Crabtree Publishing
386 Mt. Alexander Rd.
Ascot Vale (Melbourne)
VIC 3032

Contents

Chapter 1

How to Live Forever 4

Chapter 2

In the Beginning 6

Chapter 3

Animal Cell Science 14

Chapter 4

Related Research 34

Chapter 5

In the Future 40

Notebook 44

For Further Information and Web Sites 45

Glossary 46

Index 48

How to Live Forever

John Sperling founded the University of Phoenix, the nation's largest private university. This multi-millionaire then started investing in something quite small—animal cells. The research he has funded may someday have huge payoffs.

Sperling read a study about **genes**. A gene in worms seemed to allow the animals to live much longer than they would without it. Sperling wanted humans to be able to live longer, too. So he funded research to see if the same gene would help people live longer if it were put into human cells. He has since hired a group of scientists to find other ways to improve the human life span and end human suffering.

John Sperling's many interests include genetics.

You truly are seeing double with these photos. Missy, the dog, has been cloned.

One famous project involved his dog Missy. Sperling loved Missy. He could not imagine liking another dog as much. So while she was alive and well, he looked into **cloning** Missy, or making a genetic copy of her. With scientists at Texas A & M University, he started the Genetic Savings and Clone. It works like a bank for animal cells. Dog owners can send in skin cells from their pets. The company is keeping the animal cells until cloning is perfected. The cost is $1,000 up front and $100 per year until the cells are used or destroyed.

The science of animal cells, including human cells, is fascinating. As we learn more about it, the findings are changing life as we know it.

Diamond Dog

John Sperling decided to clone his dog Missy. After more than 10 years and $20 million, Missy's cells finally produced three puppies. The cost of cloning a pet is about $250,000 today. That cost is in addition to the $1,000-plus that you must pay for cell storage.

Chapter 2

In the Beginning

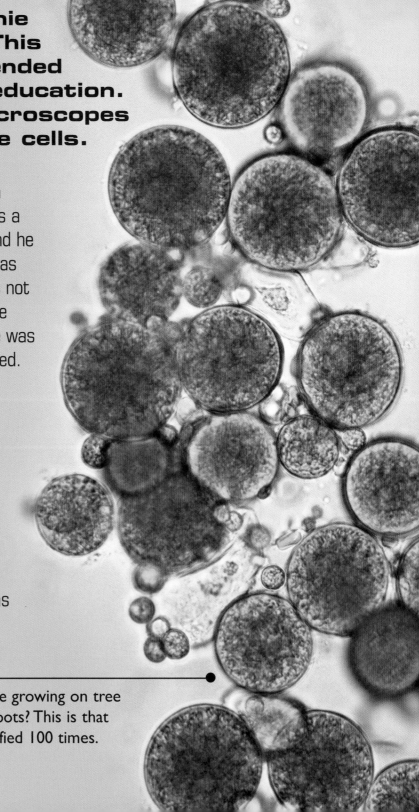

The study of cells owes a lot to Antonie van Leeuwenhoek. This scientist never attended any type of higher education. Yet he improved microscopes enough to see inside cells.

Leeuwenhoek (1632–1723) lived in Denmark, attending local schools as a child. His mother made baskets, and he grew up working with fabrics. He was extremely curious. Because he was not part of the university system, where sponsors controlled the studies, he was able to learn and study as he pleased.

Leeuwenhoek read a book that described a variety of things at close range. The scientific book inspired him. He had worked as a land surveyor, so he knew how to make lenses to see into the distance. He used this skill to make lenses for seeing close up. Leeuwenhoek was an excellent lens grinder. His microscopes could magnify objects up to 200 times.

Have you seen algae growing on tree trunks and flower pots? This is that kind of algae magnified 100 times.

The microscope spurred Leeuwenhoek's curiosity. He put anything he could under his lenses, and he made detailed observations. He was not much of an illustrator, and he needed drawings of what he saw. So he hired someone to draw what he placed under the microscope.

Leeuwenhoek wrote letters to the Royal Society of London, describing his observations. He observed insects, fossils, algae, rocks, and even the gunk that grew on his teeth. He was likely the first person to study animal cells in depth. Scientists eventually made the connection between the things he observed and animal cells, though it took a hundred years.

Hundreds of Times Better
Antonie van Leeuwenhoek gets much credit for inventing the microscope. However, scientists created the first microscopes about 40 years before he was born. Where did the confusion come from? Probably because Leeuwenhoek's microscopes were much better than anyone else's. His microscopes could magnify objects many more times than any other microscope of the time.

Sense of 'Humor'

There were plenty of odd theories about animals before animal cells were understood. Ancient philosophers believed in four **humors**. Each humor was a fluid in the body that caused illness. Other early scientists thought that animals were filled with "globules" or "little animalcules."

Yellow phlegm, bile, regular phlegm, and blood were the four humors.

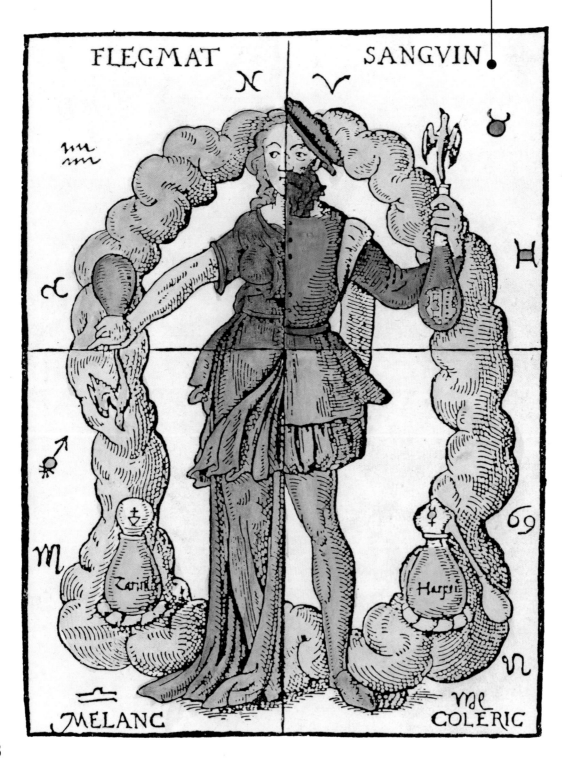

Discovering Animal Cells

Theodor Schwann published a paper in 1839 stating that every part of an animal is made of cells. He is often credited as founder of the theory of the cellular structure of animal organisms. The problem is that Jan Purkinje had already made this discovery. Purkinje came up with the same idea in 1837. When Schwann published his papers, he gave no credit to Purkinje.

Either way, by the mid-1800s, scientists understood that many different kinds of cells make up an animal's body. Scientists understood this about plants already. In order to prove the same about animals, scientists had to have the right tools. Once Leeuwenhoek's microscope was widely available, scientists could observe animal cells more closely.

Seeing and Believing

With their new close-up view, scientists collected and cataloged samples of animal **tissues**. They examined tissues under the microscope, described what they saw, and drew pictures. They studied **embryos** and recorded how all animals start out as a small group of cells.

Scientists noted how the embryo cells multiplied and eventually formed special tissues. This is how both Schwann and Purkinje came to declare that all animal tissue is made of special cells.

Connecting the Cells

Theodor Schwann was the first to connect plant and animal cells and state that cells are the basic structure of both plants and animals. In this case, he was not stating another scientist's idea. All living things use cells as building blocks. Plant cells and animal cells are similar in many ways.

Lessons in Multiplication

Scientists established that cells are the basis of animal life. Then they moved on to the next big question—How do cells reproduce? The old ideas about cells no longer made sense. In ancient Greece, Aristotle had developed the theory of **spontaneous generation**. He said that living creatures came out of substances where they were found. He believed, for example, that flies formed out of decaying meat.

Aristotle's idea sounds crazy to us now. Yet in his time, he was using his skills of observation, just as scientists do today. When an animal was killed and its body decayed, flies appeared. If Aristotle had been given the tools that later scientists had, he probably would have come up with different explanations.

In 1668, Francesco Redi proved that a living creature came only from its own kind. He declared that all animal life came from eggs. The eggs came from the same kind of animal that hatched from them.

It was once thought mice grew from rotting cheese or bread. We know better today.

Rudolf Virchow

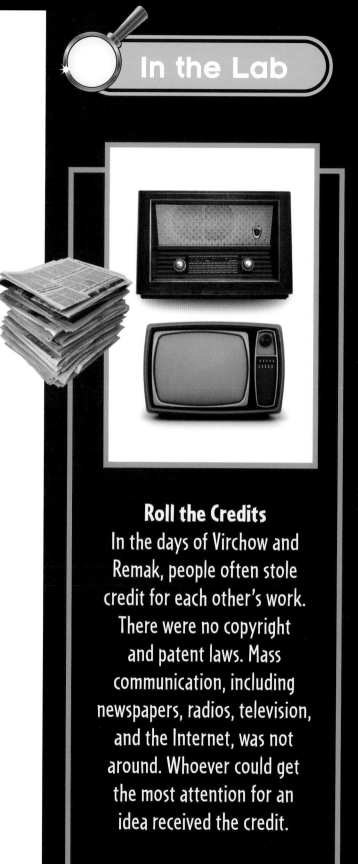

Roll the Credits
In the days of Virchow and Remak, people often stole credit for each other's work. There were no copyright and patent laws. Mass communication, including newspapers, radios, television, and the Internet, was not around. Whoever could get the most attention for an idea received the credit.

In 1850, Robert Remak published the idea that cells divide to create new cells. This idea caused a scandal in the science world. People were shocked by this "crazy" talk. Remak lost his job as a professor. He received little credit as the great scientist he was.

Rudolf Virchow had more power in the scientific community. He argued against cell division until at least 1854. Then he started arguing for the idea. Virchow studied different types of cells, including blood and cancer cells. Using what he had seen and read, he published his own papers about cell division. He used many of Remak's ideas but did not give him credit.

Bigger and Better

For a long time, Leeuwenhoek's microscope was the best tool for studying cells. Leeuwenhoek's microscope used light to focus on an object. Over the years, researchers had made many scientific discoveries with **light microscopes**. Yet cells are so small that much of their inner workings remained mysterious.

That changed around 1931. That year, Max Knoll and Ernst Ruska earned the Nobel Prize for Physics for the invention of the **electron microscope**. With Knoll and Ruska's microscope, they were able to view objects at 400 times the normal size. The new microscope did not use regular light. Instead, the microscope used electrons, the charged particles that surround **atoms**. Electrons are the particles that create electricity. The better a microscope can focus a beam of electrons, the larger the image.

Light microscopes like this one are still in use.

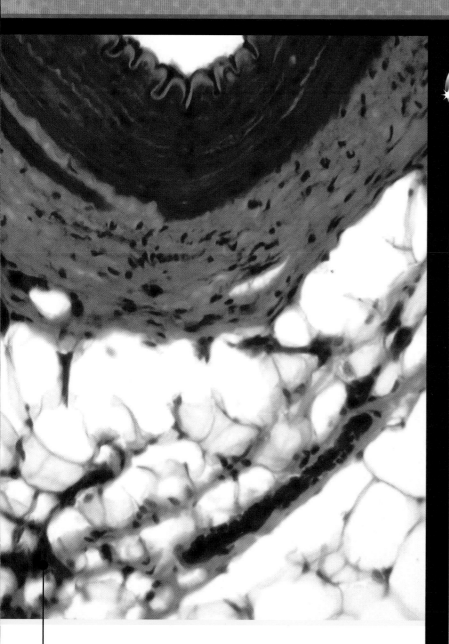

A microscope peers inside tissue taken from a dog's intestines.

Today's best light microscope can make an object appear 2,000 times larger than normal. A modern electron microscope can enlarge images by up to two million times. This means an electron microscope can give views that are 1,000 times larger than that of a light microscope. These new microscopes led to a boom in the study of cells. Suddenly scientists could see the smallest of cells. They could study the smallest parts inside cells.

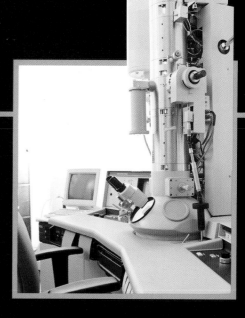

Looks Could Kill

Light microscopes were the only microscopes available for more than 300 years. These tools were great for looking at tiny organisms. Yet they could not enlarge an image enough to see everything inside a cell. Electron microscopes could magnify images many more times. There was one large problem, however. The powerful blast of electrons killed the cells being viewed.

Chapter 3

Animal Cell Science

Scientists have learned that cells are like businesses that specialize, or do work in one area. A grocery store sells groceries, but not parts for your computer. By specializing, businesses become better at the things they do. Animal cells specialize, too.

Animal cells are one type of **eukaryote**. Cells that have a **nucleus** are eukaryotes. These cells become specialized and often perform only one job. For example, all of the cells that know how to protect the outside of your body form skin tissue.

Eukaryotes have nuclei and other **organelles**. The organelles are structures that help the cell live and do its job. Plants and animals are made of eukaryotic cells. When new plants or animals are formed, the cells multiply and grow. Quite quickly, the cells understand the kinds of tissue they will become, and the cells start doing those jobs. Because of this, all plants and animals have many cells and many types of tissue.

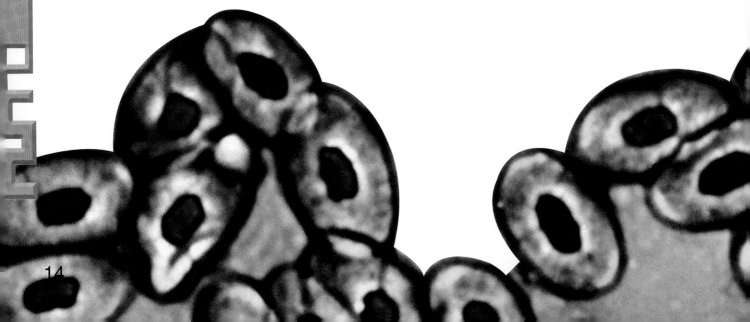

There are also many cells that have no nucleus and are not eukaryotes. These cells are called **prokaryotes**. **Bacteria** are prokaryotes. Bacteria have no specialized tissues. Prokaryotes cannot organize and become creatures that are more complex.

Plant and animal cells are all eukaryotes. Yet that does not mean their cells are alike, any more than the plants and animals themselves are alike. Plants do not have livers. Hummingbirds cannot make their own food. The differences between plants and animals reach all the way to the cellular level.

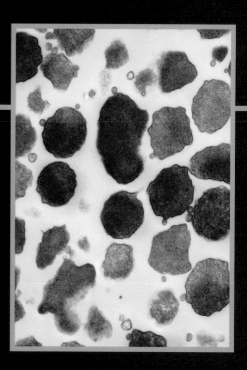

The nuclei of these red blood cells, taken from a frog, are in clear view.

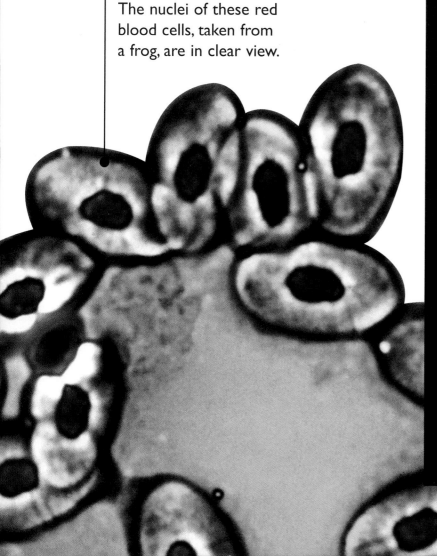

Speak Greek
Prokaryote and *eukaryote* come from Greek roots. The Greek word *karyon* means "nut." Nuts are types of seeds. In many ways, they look like cells. The prefix *eu* - means "good" or "well." *Pro* - means "before." If you put the prefix and root together, you get a hint of which type of cell scientists think came first.

15

See Inside an Animal Cell

The **cell membrane** holds the animal cell together. The membrane is flexible. Different animal cells have different shapes, and the cells can change shape as needed. The membrane is also porous. This means it can let substances in and out of the cell. Substances going into the cell usually provide nutrients. Substances going out of the cell could be waste or other chemicals.

The **cytoplasm** has the texture of jelly and holds the organelles inside the cell in place. It also takes up most of the space inside a cell. The cytoplasm works like a shock absorber. If the cell is bumped, the cytoplasm keeps the other organelles from bumping one another. The cytoplasm also holds material going in and out of the cell until it gets to where it is supposed to be. The nucleus of each cell serves as the "brain" of the cell. The nucleus has instructions that tell the cell what to do and when to do it. It also has all of the cell's hereditary information.

A **mitochondrion** is a small power factory. The mitochondria take nutrients from the cell and turn them into energy. This process is called **cellular respiration**. A cell that needs a lot of energy can have thousands of mitochondria. Cells that need less energy can have far fewer of these organelles. If a cell needs more energy, it can make more mitochondria.

You Are Busy

Humans can have as many as 100,000,000,000,000 or 100 trillion cells! Each cell knows how to take in nutrients, change them to energy, perform a special job, and make more cells when they are needed. All of this happens without your thinking about it.

The organelle with the biggest name is the **endoplasmic reticulum**. Most scientists just call it the ER. In some ways, the ER is like a delivery service. It takes materials from the cytoplasm and carries them to the organelles that need them. The ER also provides an inspection service. If material made by the cell is made incorrectly, the ER sends it back. If material coming into the cell is not made correctly, the ER keeps it from going any further. ER can either be rough or smooth.

One Tissue, Many Cells

Human cells and other kinds of animal cells specialize in important ways. For example, some cells work together to form the human liver. However, not every cell in an organ is the same. The outside of the liver is like skin, but the inside is not. The cells located in both of those spots are different.

Four Types of Cells

Biologists have classified animal cells in four different categories: **epithelial**, **connective**, **muscle**, and **nerve**. When you think about all of the jobs the organs in your body have, it is amazing that the cells fall into only four groups.

Epithelial cells make up the covering and lining of organs. Skin is epithelial tissue. So is the outside of your organs. Epithelial cells let substances in and out of the organs. For example, your skin can soak in medicine, and it can sweat.

Hair cells are actually dead cells that have been bound with a kind of protein.

Epithelial cells also provide protection. Skin, for example, protects the insides of your body.

You can find connective cells just under the layer of epithelial cells. You can find other connective cells in bones. The connective cells store fat and give further protection to the body. The space they take up absorbs energy that could injure you.

Muscle cells move. The muscles found close to bones are made of large cells. Smaller muscle cells make up much of the heart. These cells use a tremendous amount of energy in order to move all parts of an animal.

Nerve cells look like strings. They send and receive signals throughout the body. The cells communicate through chemicals and electricity that move from cell to cell.

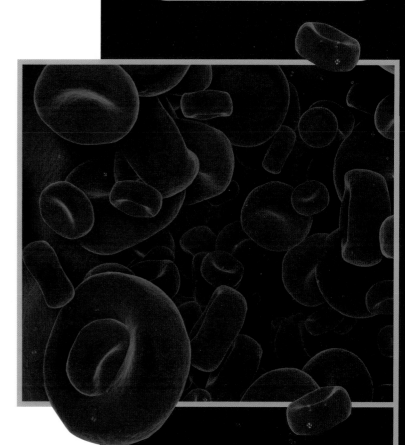

Connective cells also make the tissue that binds muscle to bone.

Connected by Blood
Even though blood is a fluid, it is connective tissue. The other connective tissues are not liquid. Other connective cells are more like string or fiber, which makes them more solid. Insects also have a liquid connective tissue. The liquid tissue carries nutrients into other cells of the body and takes waste away.

Information Central

The nucleus of each cell contains the cell's hereditary information and controls the cell's activities. The hereditary information is called **deoxyribonucleic acid** or **DNA**. The DNA gives instructions for new cells when the original cell multiplies.

A Closer Look

A nuclear envelope surrounds the nucleus. The envelope works like the cell membrane, letting material in and out of the nucleus. The nuclear envelope has pores, much like your skin does. The pores allow material to move in and out of the nucleus from the cytoplasm.

The nucleus is packed with DNA. The DNA has all of the information that a cell passes down to its offspring. For example, if an animal has blue eyes, it is because the DNA in the cells of its eyes says blue is the right color.

Inside the nuclear envelope is a material that looks like fiber. It spreads throughout the cell. This material joins with the DNA to make **chromosomes** when the cell is ready to divide. The chromosomes split into two when the cell divides. The number of chromosomes in a cell depends on the type of animal.

Researchers watch cell movement and other cell behaviors to better understand life.

The Cell Nucleus

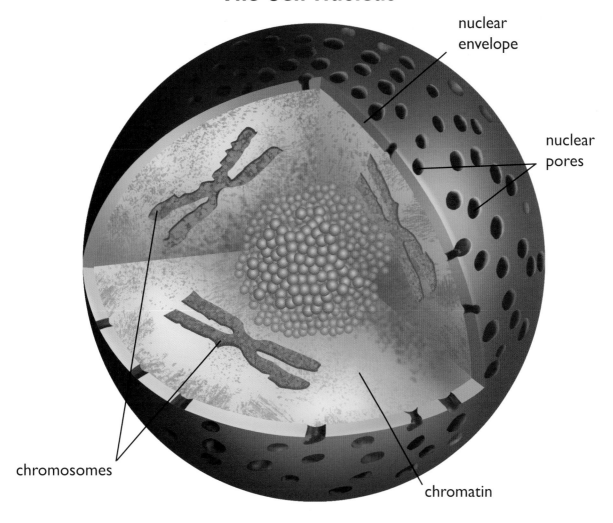

nuclear
envelope

nuclear
pores

chromosomes

chromatin

Nuclear envelope – Two layers of membrane that protect the inside of the nucleus

Nuclear pores – Openings in the nuclear membrane that allow material in and out of the nucleus

Chromatin – Fiber that fills the nucleus; mixes with DNA to form chromosomes

Chromosomes – Genetic instructions from the parent cell, given to the offspring when cells divide

Central Mystery

Even with advances in technology, scientists do not know everything that happens in a nucleus. As late as 2006, no college textbooks could accurately describe a nucleus. Just because biologists can see inside a nucleus does not mean they *understand* it.

Scientists have seen chromosomes. Researchers have measured DNA. In each human cell the length of the DNA, if it could be set end-to-end, would be many feet or meters long. Yet the DNA packs up so tightly that it fits inside a microscopic space. How is this possible?

Another mystery surrounds **junk DNA**. Biologists have studied many types of DNA over the last few decades. These researchers know what some of the DNA controls, but they do not know what all DNA does. DNA that they do not recognize has been called junk DNA. This does not mean that the mysterious DNA is useless. Chances are, the opposite is true. We just do not know the role of junk DNA in animal life yet.

This artistic rendering of DNA highlights its **double helix** shape. DNA is formed like a twisted ladder. The rungs are pairings of chemicals called bases. The sides are made of atoms of sugar and phosphate.

Scientists have also discovered DNA outside of the nucleus. Some DNA is in the mitochondria. Under close inspection, it is clear that the DNA in mitochondria is not the same as the DNA in the nucleus. There is evidence that the mitochondria DNA is related to bacteria. How did this other form of DNA get inside so many animal cells?

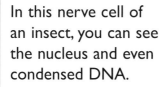

In this nerve cell of an insect, you can see the nucleus and even condensed DNA.

$$I = \int_0^{\pi} \frac{x \sin x}{1 + \cos^2 x}\, dx$$

Counting on Cells
Mathematicians work with biologists to understand where DNA is located in the nucleus. The mathematicians take measurements and find patterns that tell how the inside of a nucleus is structured. Math is a way to describe things with numbers.

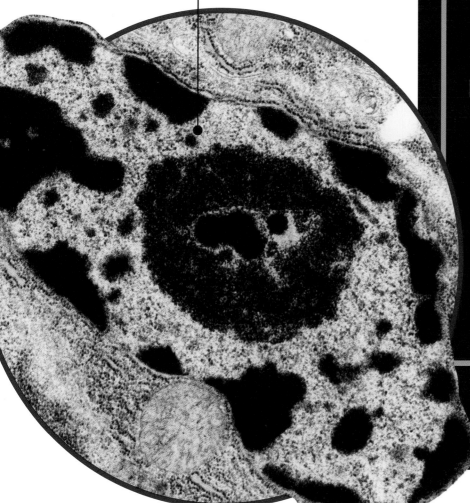

Divide and Multiply

At some point, nearly any cell has to replace itself. An embryo cell splits so that the embryo grows. Cells also split to replace old or damaged cells. In a human, this process of **mitosis** can take just 30 to 90 minutes.

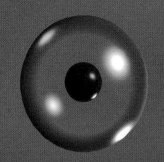

Mothers and Daughters

In mitosis, the cell makes two exact copies of itself. The parent cell is the mother. The offspring cells are daughters. The only animal cells that do not go through mitosis are sperm and eggs, the cells that create a new animal. Sperm and eggs split in another way.

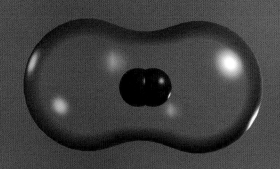

Mitosis is essentially division of the nucleus. The nucleus has the genetic information that must be copied and divided.

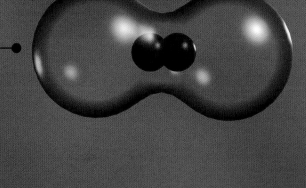

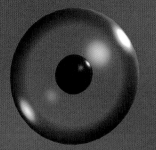
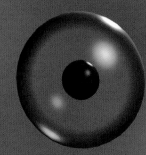

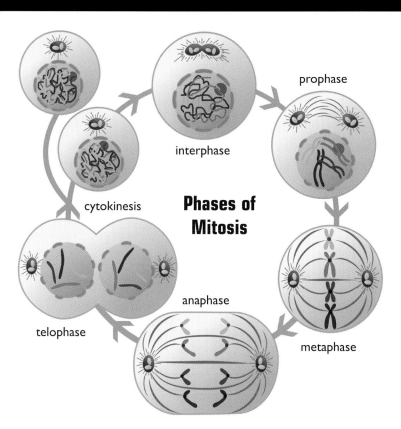

Phases of Mitosis

prophase

interphase

cytokinesis

telophase

anaphase

metaphase

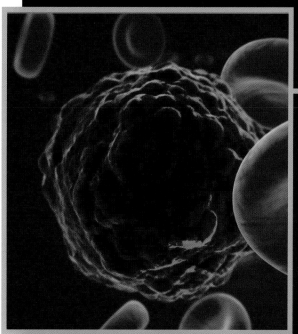

Looks Like Cancer
Healthy human cells can be grown in a lab in a flat layer. The cells stop growing as soon as they touch another cell. Cancer cells do not stay in a flat layer when they grow in a lab. They do not stop growing when they touch other cells. This gives doctors a simple way to tell cancer cells from healthy cells.

1. **Prophase** DNA shortens and thickens to form chromosomes. The nuclear membrane disappears. The **centrioles** move to opposite ends of the cell.

2. **Metaphase** Long fibers extend from the centrioles and attach themselves to the chromosomes. The chromosomes line up in the center of the cell.

3. **Anaphase** The fibers shorten and pull the chromosomes apart. The chromosomes begin to move toward opposite ends of the cell.

4. **Telophase** The chromosomes reach the opposite ends of the cell. The nuclear membrane reappears around each new nucleus. The long fibers disappear.

Cytokinesis comes next. The cell splits apart and becomes two sister cells.

Making Mini Me

Just like cells can make replicas of themselves, so can entire animals. In mitosis, one mother cell becomes two daughter cells. The daughter cells are exactly like the mother cell. In **asexual reproduction**, the parent creates offspring identical to the parent.

Coral, which live in the sea, reproduce by **budding**. That is a process in which a new animal grows on a parent animal's body. In some cases, the offspring stays attached to the parent. In a coral colony, the animals grow one onto another. Jellyfish can also reproduce by budding. In most cases, the bud breaks off the parent and survives on its own.

Coral reproduce asexually through budding. They can reproduce by releasing eggs and sperm into the water, too.

Another form of asexual reproduction is **fragmentation**. Many types of worms can break into many parts. Each part can then grow into a new worm, exactly like the parent. Some sponges can reproduce this way, too.

A few animals can create offspring through **regeneration**. You may have seen animals that can lose a body part and survive, such as when a sea star loses a limb. In animals such as sea stars, body parts can have enough cells to create a whole new animal.

Finally, some types of fish, lizards, and insects are all female. These animals reproduce through **parthenogenesis**. The female lays an egg, and the egg develops into an animal. The female never mates.

When a sea star loses a limb, it grows a new one, thanks to cell division.

In the Lab

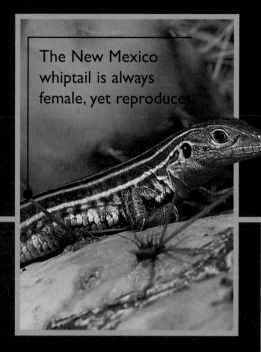

The New Mexico whiptail is always female, yet reproduces.

Problem Parents

There are many advantages to asexual reproduction, as opposed to reproduction between males and females. It does not take as long to create offspring. It also takes little energy from the parent. It eliminates the need for finding a mate, which can be a problem. The one-parent method can create many more offspring than can the two-parent process.

Meiosis I begins. The cell copies its own DNA.

interphase

prophase I

metaphase I

anaphase I

telophase I

cytokinesis I

Meiosis

Animals, including humans, have special cells called **gametes**. The male gamete is a sperm. The female gamete is an egg. Each gamete has only half the number of chromosomes that an animal cell needs. When the gametes combine, the new cell has all the chromosomes needed.

The process of **meiosis** creates gametes. Meiosis has two cell divisions rather than one. Yet the DNA splits only once. This means one mother cell ends up making four daughters. The gametes have half the normal number of chromosomes and are not identical to the parent. Meiosis I begins as the cell makes a copy of its DNA.

1. **Prophase I** DNA shortens and thickens to form chromosomes. Pairs of similar chromosomes line up tightly beside each other. The nuclear membrane disappears. Centrioles move to opposite ends of the cell.

2. **Metaphase I** Long fibers extend from the centrioles and attach themselves to the chromosomes. The chromosomes line up in the center of the cell.

3. **Anaphase I** The fibers shorten and pull one of the matching pairs of chromosomes toward opposite ends of the cell.

4. **Telophase I** The movement is complete. Each end of the cell has 23 chromosomes. The nuclear membrane reappears around each new nucleus. The long fibers disappear.

5. **Cytokinesis** The cell splits into two **haploid cells**. Notice at this point that the chromosomes do not duplicate again.

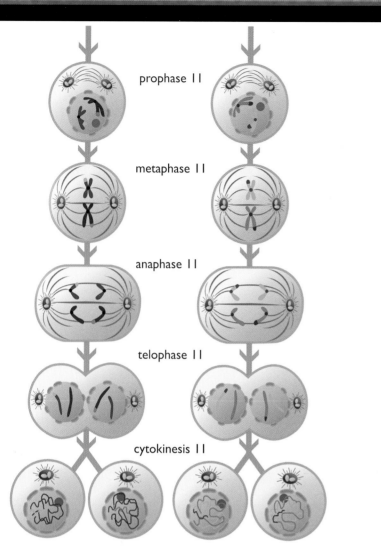

prophase II

metaphase II

anaphase II

telophase II

cytokinesis II

Me and Mi
Mitosis and *meiosis* are spelled similarly and have some similar phases. How can you keep them straight? Remember that *mitosis* has an IT that can stand for "Identical Twins." *Meiosis* has an E and an S that can stand for "Egg" and "Sperm."

Meiosis II comes next:

6. **Prophase II** The nuclear membranes in both cells disappear again. The centrioles move to opposite ends of each of the cells.

7. **Metaphase II** Long fibers extend from the centrioles and attach themselves to the chromosomes. The chromosomes line up in the center of the cell.

8. **Anaphase II** The fibers shorten and pull the chromosomes apart. The chromosomes begin to move toward opposite ends of the cell.

9. **Telophase II** The chromosomes reach the opposite ends of the cell. The nuclear membrane reappears around each new nucleus. The long fibers disappear.

10. **Cytokinesis** The cell splits apart. There are now four daughter cells, each with only 23 chromosomes.

Simple Animals

Animals come in many shapes and forms. Some of these creatures are very complex. Think about a chameleon. A chameleon can not only think, hunt, eat, and reproduce; it can also change color. Other animals are simple. Some do not even move. Yet they eat, grow, and reproduce.

Sponges and Cnidarians

Sponges live at the bottom of the ocean. Most attach themselves to some hard surface, such as a rock. Then they take in nourishment from the water and debris on the ocean floor. Some sponges are quite small. Others can grow much larger. The barrel sponge, for example, is big enough for a person to fit inside of it.

The cells on the outside of a sponge protect the animal from dangers in the water.

Sponges are animals, so that means they have specialized cells. One type of cell is found in the outer covering. Another type of cell is found inside the creature. These cells take in nutrients when water flows through the sponge. Many sponges are simple. You could pull one apart, piece by piece, and any part with both types of cells could turn into a new sponge.

Sponges are called filter feeders. They draw water in and filter out the food. Filter feeders help people monitor the environment. If the water is polluted, the sponges will suffer. People can use this as a signal that there is a problem.

Cnidarians have cells that are similar to sponge cells. In addition to the outer covering and inner cells, cnidarians also have mouths and tentacles, a kind of arm. The tentacles let these animals swim through the water and capture prey. Jellyfish are a type of cnidarian. These simple, yet amazing, animals can reproduce asexually or sexually.

Jellyfish have more kinds of cells than sponges do.

One Old Sponge
Sponges may have been one of the earliest animals to develop on Earth. How do we know? The oldest producing oil field in the world (in Oman, east of Saudi Arabia) has chemicals that can be linked to sponges. These early sponges probably lived about 600 million years ago.

Complex Animals

We know many examples of animals far more complex than sponges and cnidarians. You, for one! Humans are complex animals. Whales and house cats are, too. They have many more types of tissue than sponges and jellyfish. There are other traits that make animals complex, too.

The Four Traits

Complex animals have four traits in common. One of those traits is **bilateral body symmetry.** Look at yourself in a mirror. What if you drew a line straight down the middle from the top of your head? The two sides of your body look like mirror images. Where you have one eye, another is on the other side. You have one arm and one leg on each side. Other animals are the same, whether they live on land or in the water.

Can you see bilateral body symmetry in both?

32

Complex animals also develop a brain and some sort of spine. Many animals with a nervous system are easy to spot. They have heads! Think about the jellyfish. It has no head, and no real brain. This is part of why a jellyfish is not a complex animal.

In addition, complex animals have a body cavity. A body cavity is a space under the skin where organs develop. Humans have many body cavities. The head is a cavity for the brain. The abdomen is a cavity for the stomach, liver, kidneys, and more. We have another cavity for the lungs and heart.

Finally, the cells of complex animals specialize. All complex animals have many different types of cells, from the neurons in the brain to the white blood cells that fight disease.

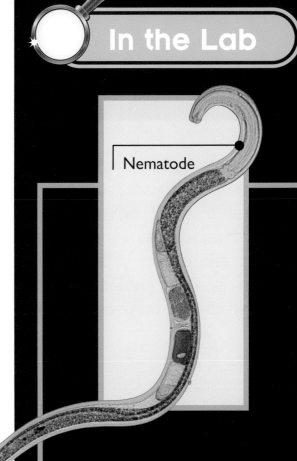

Nematode

Big Brain
The scientific word for developing a nervous system is **cephalization**. Understanding the root of the word makes it simple. The Latin word *cephalicus* means "skull." Hydrocephalus is a condition with too much fluid (*hydro-* means "water") on the brain. Encephalitis is swelling of the brain.

Neurons have branches called dendrites. They work like antennae.

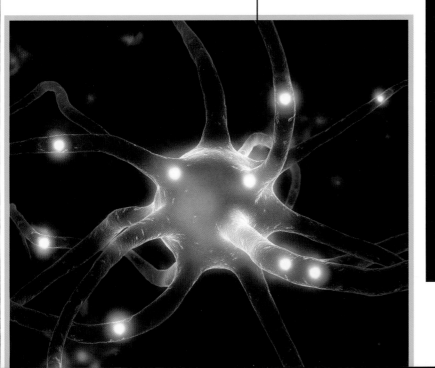

Chapter 4

Related Research

When parents are expecting, they guess what the baby will be like. "Will she have your eyes?" "I hope he has your hair!" "Will he be able to play piano like Grandma?" Parents pass some traits on to children through DNA.

Some of a parent's traits are expressed in the offspring. Other traits can be passed along in the genes but stay hidden. The DNA in the nucleus of a cell carries the information or code about traits. The gametes made in meiosis are the cells that create offspring. It is the gametes that carry along the DNA that controls the traits that the offspring inherit. Each gamete has an **allele** for each trait. In humans, for example, each parent has an allele that determines whether the child will have dimples. The allele for dimples does not control other characteristics. Two alleles, one from the mother and one from the father, combine in the new human.

The allele for having a cleft chin is dominant.

Pea pods provided important clues in early genetic studies.

Every set of alleles gives instructions for one trait. The combined alleles give directions saying whether or not dimples will show up.

Alleles can be **dominant** or **recessive**. The trait for dimples is dominant. This means a baby needs only one dimple allele to be born with dimples. The trait for "no dimples" is recessive. A recessive trait needs to be the same in both alleles in order to appear. A baby with the "no dimples" allele from both parents would not have dimples.

Like Peas in a Pod

Dominant and recessive traits were discovered by Gregor Mendel in the 1800s. Mendel studied pea pods. He noted how the color of flowers and pea pods passed from parent to offspring.

A Test You Can't Fail

If you have ever watched talk shows, soap operas, or crime dramas, you have seen people use DNA tests to identify a person or tell if two people are related. Doctors first used DNA tests in the 1980s.

DNA testing is another name for genetic testing. Today genetic testing can do far more than tell if two people are related. Genetic testing can give you information about your ancestry. For example, DNA can show that a person's ancestors lived in a region of Central Africa many hundreds of years ago.

Genetic testing is making advances in medicine as well. Tests can show if a person or other animal has a genetic disease. Tests tell if the animal carries the gene for a genetic disease or might develop a disease. Genetic testing can even determine the best dose of medicine for a particular disease.

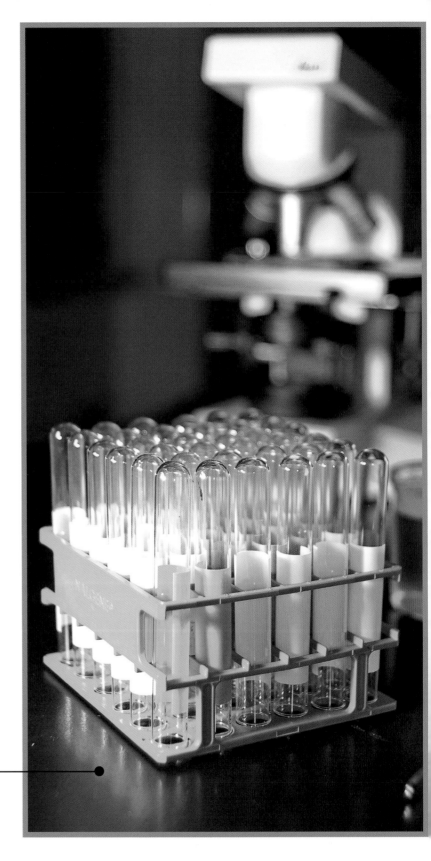

DNA testing has countless applications in life beyond the lab.

A researcher views data for a DNA fingerprint.

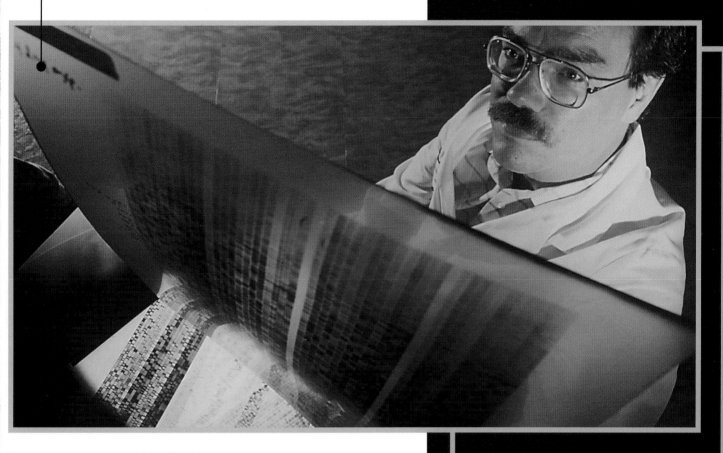

Doctors can test babies both before and after birth. Doctors can take cells from the baby as it grows in the mother's womb. The cells can show whether the baby will be born with severe diseases. Knowing this ahead of time lets parents prepare to care for the baby. After the baby is born, genetic testing can show if the infant is missing genes. Testing tells if the child has genes that will cause problems doctors would not see otherwise.

Detectives can now use DNA to match evidence at crime scenes with the criminals that commit the crimes. DNA can come from any human cell. Hair or even fingernail clippings can lead detectives to criminals.

Map of Me

One person's entire set of DNA is a **genome**. One person has an average of 30,000 genes. The Human Genome Project shows a map of all of the genes that may be found in a human. Scientists know what those genes are. Now they have to figure out what all of them do.

Expensive Genes

If you go to a pet store, a Chihuahua may cost $500.
At a pet shelter, a mutt can cost less than $50.
Why are the costs so different?

Purebreds

Purebred animals are animals that have the same breed
of parents, grandparents, and so on. So the Chihuahua
in the pet store, if it is purebred, has Chihuahua parents,
Chihuahua grandparents, and Chihuahua great-grandparents.
The dog is pure Chihuahua. Dog owners who buy a purebred
want to be sure that the animal they buy has only the genes
for the breed they want.

Dogs are not the only animal in which purebreds can
matter to people. Cat and horse owners sometimes want
purebreds, too. The traits of a specific breed appeal to
owners. Many animal shows allow only purebreds to
compete. For example, the Westminster Dog Show allows
purebred dogs to compete against each other. The contest
rewards the dog that best shows the traits of the breed.

Leopard-spotted
Appaloosas are
especially prized.

Dalmations have many positive traits but carry a gene for deafness.

This does not mean that purebred animals are better than mixed-breed animals. As a matter of fact, many purebred animals suffer because they are purebred. Dalmatians are beautiful dogs. Yet purebred Dalmatians have a greater risk of being deaf than mixed breeds. The genes in these dogs developed errors over time. This flawed gene passes from parent to puppy again and again. More Dalmatians carry the deafness gene, so there is a better chance that a Dalmatian puppy will be deaf. Many other purebred animals suffer from medical problems that are in their genes.

Mix and Match
If you have a mixed-breed dog, you can find out its breed or breeds. Just like your DNA can tell about your ancestors, the dog's DNA can tell whether the dog comes from a poodle or Pekinese. Animal DNA testing also helps vets treat diseases in cats, dogs, horses, and other animals.

Chapter 5

In the Future

Have you ever used modeling clay?
If so, you know that you can create
just about anything with it. Most living
things start out with cells that are
like a kind of modeling clay. They can be
shaped into whatever the being needs.

Stem cells were first
discovered in the 1960s
by Canadian scientists.

All the cells in the human body have a specialized function. There are brain cells, blood cells, and many others. Each performs a certain job. Yet they did not start out that way. All humans, and in fact, nearly all organisms, start out with basic building blocks called **stem cells**.

A stem cell has two key properties. First, it has self-renewal. This means that it can go through mitosis and continue being a stem cell. Second, it can transform into a mature cell with a specialized function.

There are two types of stems cells, but they are similar. Embryonic stem cells are present in the first stages of an organism's life. These cells can become any other type of cell that the organism needs. There are also adult stem cells, which are in the tissues of mature organisms. For example, a person's liver contains liver cells and liver stem cells. These stem cells are activated when a liver cell is damaged or dies. The organ is renewed and can continue to function.

Lately, stem cells have become an active field for research. The results have led to groundbreaking medical treatments. Doctors successfully use bone marrow stem cells to fight leukemia, a cancer affecting the blood. In the future, scientists believe they will be able to treat multiple sclerosis, Parkinson's disease, and many other conditions.

In the Lab

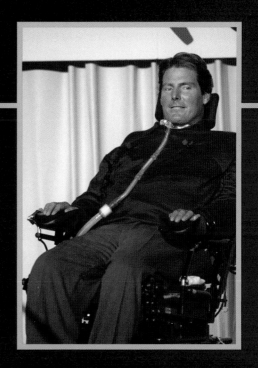

Truly Superman
After suffering a terrible spinal cord injury, actor Christopher Reeve decided to pour all of his resources into researching treatment for his paralysis. He and his wife formed the Christopher and Dana Reeve Foundation. The organization has funded more than $60 million of research, including treatment using spinal cord stem cells.

The Nature of Things

Imagine twin brothers who are separated at birth. One grows up in a desert country. The other is raised near the Arctic Circle. After many years, they might end up looking quite different from each other.

The differences between the twins might be explained by **epigenetics**. This science looks at how an animal's DNA is changed by its environment. *Epi* is from a Greek word meaning "over" or "above." In other words, where an animal grows up or lives might affect its genetic makeup. A specific gene could be "expressed," or behave differently under different environmental conditions.

Even people who appear identical do not have identical genes.

An animal's DNA is a lot like a computer program. It has thousands of lines of code called genes that can be turned on or turned off. Scientists have studied many of these genes to determine what affects the genes over time. They have discovered some genes that cause specific diseases.

Many diseases, such as cancer, are successful because they suppress a gene's immune system. Yet in one case, scientists have discovered how to help genes fight back. The drug azacitidine was developed to help genes "turn on" their defenses against leukemia. These treatments involve some risk, however. While helping genes in one way, the drugs also might be changing them in unexpected ways.

Researchers are making a map of all the changes that can occur to genes. Using this map, they can develop new treatments. They may also discover how certain habits can affect a person's genetic makeup. Can you think of ways this research will help you and your family?

In the Lab

Finding All Factors
Scientists have discovered about 22,000 genes. In order to study epigenetics thoroughly, scientists have to study how every environmental and behavioral change impacts each and every gene. Scientists will be busy for many years to come, and that is just in the area of human epigenetics.

Notebook

Science Fair

Use foods in your kitchen to make a model of an animal cell. Ask an adult to help you.

Materials:

- a resealable, gallon-size plastic bag
- gelatin dessert mix
- water
- large bowl
- small grapes
- 2-4 small Mandarin orange segments
- cooked lasagna noodles

Method:

1. Open a plastic bag and set it on a table or countertop.
2. Follow the instructions on the box of gelatin to make the dessert. Use the large bowl and water as the box directs.
3. Pour the gelatin in the plastic bag.
4. Add materials or "organelles" to the bag.
5. Seal the bag and place your cell in the refrigerator. It will take several hours for the gelatin to firm up.
6. Use the diagram on pages 16-17 to identify the parts of your cell model.

For Further Information

Books

Snedden, Robert. **Animals**: **Multicelled Life**. Mankato, Minnesota: Heinemann Library, 2008.

Stille, Darlene P. **Animal Cells: Smallest Units of Life**. Mankato, Minnesota: Compass Point Books, 2006.

Walker, Richard. **Kingfisher Knowledge Genes and DNA**. London: Kingfisher, 2007.

Web sites

www.amnh.org/ology/?channel=genetics&cbiology4kids.com

www.biology4kids.com

www.howstuffworks.com/genetic-science/missyplicity.htm

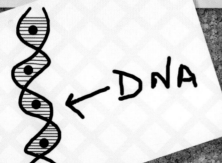

←DNA

The problem with the gene pool is that there's no lifeguard.

David Gerrold
(1944–present, sci-fi author)

Glossary

allele Different forms of the same gene, which determines a trait

asexual reproduction Formation of a new organism with cells from only one parent

atoms Smallest building blocks of living and nonliving things

bacteria Type of prokaryotic organism

bilateral body symmetry The quality of a body to have line symmetry

budding Asexual reproduction in which offspring come from an outgrowth of the parent

cell membrane Outer barrier of an animal cell that allows materials to pass in and out

cells Smallest units that make up every living thing

cellular respiration Breaking down food and exchanging carbon dioxide for oxygen

centrioles Organelles in animal cells needed for cell division

cephalization Development of a nervous system

chromosomes Coiled threads of DNA containing genes

cloning Creating a second genetically identical being

connective cells Cells that store fat and protect organs in the body

cytokinesis A stage of cell changes in mitosis, meiosis, and fertilization

cytoplasm Jelly-like substance found inside the cell membrane

deoxyribonucleic acid (DNA) Long strand of genetic information found in a cell's nucleus

dominant The trait that will show itself even if it is on only one chromosome

double helix Spiral consisting of two strands of DNA, resembles the shape of a spiral staircase

electron microscope A tool for viewing small substances by using a beam of electrons instead of light

embryos Undeveloped animals

endoplasmic reticulum (ER) Series of canals, like veins, running through the cell

epigenetics Having to do with the effects of the environment on an organism's genes

epithelial cells Cells that line organs

eukaryote Organism made of cells that contain nuclei

fragmentation Asexual reproduction in which an organism breaks into parts that become like the parent

gametes Reproductive cells with half the normal genetic material

genes The parts of DNA that control inherited traits

genome The total genetic information for an organism

haploid cells Cells that contain only one copy of a chromosome set

humors Four fluids once considered to control health

junk DNA Sections of chromosomes in between genes that do not code for proteins

light microscopes Tools for viewing small substances using lenses and focused light

meiosis Type of cell division which forms the sex cells (egg and sperm)

mitochondrion An organelle that turns food into energy

mitosis Type of cell division that produces two identical cells

muscle cells Cells that allow movement

nerve cells Cells that communicate through the nervous system

nucleus Control center of plant or animal cells

organelles General name for parts of a cell

parthenogenesis Asexual reproduction of a seed, spore, or the like organisms made of cells that do not contain nuclei

prokaryotes Organisms made of cells that do not contain nuclei

recessive The trait that will show itself if the code for it is on both chromosomes

regeneration Asexual replacement of an injured or lost body part

spontaneous generation Idea that living things can arise from nonliving matter

stem cells Cells that can develop into a variety of cell types

tissues Structural materials that work together in an organism

Index

allele 34, 35
anaphase 25, 28, 29
Aristotle 10
asexual reproduction
    26, 27, 34
atoms 12

bacteria 15, 23
bilateral body symmetry
    32
budding 26

cell membrane 16, 20
cells 4–31, 33, 34, 37,
    40, 41
cellular respiration 17
centrioles 25, 28, 29
cephalization 33
chromatin 21
chromosomes 20, 21,
    22, 25, 28, 29
cloning 5
connective cells 18, 19
cytokinesis 25, 28, 29
cytoplasm 16, 17, 20

deoxyribonucleic acid (DNA)
    20-23, 25, 28, 29, 34,
    36–39, 42, 43
dominant 34, 35

electron microscope
    12, 13
embryos 9, 24
endoplasmic reticulum (ER)
    17
epigenetics 42, 43
epithelial cells 18, 19
eukaryote 14, 15

fragmentation 27

gametes 28, 34
genes 4, 34, 36–39,
    42, 43
genome 37

Human Genome Project
    37
humors 8

junk DNA 22

Knoll, Max 12

Leeuwenhoek, Antonie van
    6, 7, 9, 12
light microscopes 12, 13

meiosis 28, 29, 34
Mendel, Gregor 35
metaphase 25, 28, 29
Missy, the dog 4, 5
mitochondrion 17, 22, 23
mitosis 24–26, 41
muscle cells 18, 19

nerve cells 18, 19
nuclear envelope 20-21
nuclear pores 20-21
nucleus 14, 15, 16,
    20-25, 28, 29, 34

organelles 14-17

parthenogenesis 27
prokaryotes 15, 28, 29
prophase 25
Purkinje, Jan 9

recessive 35, 25
Redi, Francesco 10
Reeve, Christopher 41
regeneration 27
Remak, Robert 11
Royal Society of London 7
Ruska, Ernst 12

Schwann, Theodor 9
Sperling, John 4, 5
spontaneous generation 10
stem cells 40, 41

telophase 25, 28, 29
tissues 9, 14, 15, 18,
    19, 32, 41

Virchow, Rudolf 11

Printed in the U.S.A.—CG